In Search of

Moonlit Crevices

Dawnbreaker Poetry Series

~~~

Dancing Letters by Miguel Cruz
Christmas Poetry by J. E. Deegan
In Search of Moonlit Crevices by Marcel Wormsley

For a full catalog of works by Marcel
and other authors, please visit
dawnbreakerpress.com

In Search of Moonlit Crevices

Marcel Wormsley

Dawnbreaker Press

Galveston, Texas

Published by
Dawnbreaker Press
Galveston, Texas
dawnbreakerpress.com

Book design by Chandler Barton
Cover art by Elena Reznikova
Illustrations by Elena Reznikova & Olena Zavakevych

ISBN:
978-0-9992054-3-3 (paperback)
978-0-9992054-4-0 (hardcover)
978-0-9992054-5-7 (e-book)

Typeset in Calluna

First edition, 2019

A Candlelight wanes

in the breeze, but in

stillness, its strength

is replenished.

Preface

T HE TITLE OF THIS WORK refers more to the thought processes and cognitive mechanisms associated with reading the poems therein rather than any particular moment, vignette or recalled experience. Thematically, the poems themselves run the gamut of lived experience – from the deeply humanizing to the utterly transcendent – and were designed to flirt with the deepest recesses of our reflective consciousness, so that there is always some new illuminating insight to be gleaned through each successive reading.

In this case, new and hitherto unexplored fissures (perhaps neuroanatomically akin to the sulcus of the brain's surface) of our conscious awareness are always being put into view, as if by the light of a cosmic moon. Hence, the constant search for greater meaning and significance in these moonlit crevices, through waiting, and wanting, becoming: pain, ecstasy, frequent forays into a hallowed place that reason forgot in pursuit of flight, conversations with fragile noumenons that daily seep into those illuminated crevices lining the jagged path toward self-realization.

This book is a journey throughout the restless voids of space and time hidden within these crevices, a meditation on thought and thoughtlessness, on beauty for its own sake and acute desire, on the path from the gulf of despair to the brinks of redemption. It is an excursion amid the gentle undulations of hollow waves, subtle nuances of light and the direction of the imperious wind, amid impressions of being within the fullness of itself, inside and outside, through and through, until love begins to seep through the cracks.

It is a collection of moments ranging in duration but steadily reaching for an overall persistence, a kind of intuitive knowing if you will, where spontaneity has elongated itself into a panoply of restless color and movement, attempting to both fathom the abyss of grief and despair and soar into the farthest reach-

Marcel Wormsley

es of cosmic distances within the rarefied space of an eye that blinks only once for the spontaneous self-projecting beauty that remains.

In all, this work is a culmination of myriad luminous hours of reflection and immersion, of sitting beside the window most nights or vis-à-vis a moving work of art. Or of closing my eyes to the world of sensation and allowing the movement of nothingness/expansion/presence to overtake a soul that has allowed itself to be moved by the spiritual impetus of creation. I invite you to surrender with me along pathways that venture deep within the voids, beneath the words, the figures and even the very thoughts they invoke. Unravel as you journey deeper still into the crevices, and continue searching, not for meaning or rational significance, but for the very source of illumination that you had already become, many moons ago.

In Search of Moonlit Crevices

Seed

A wayward seed drifts from home
Captive for a solemn winter's night.
It emerges cautiously, begins to roam,
Vexed and bewitched by an inconstant light.

It finds solace in an array of black stones
Strewn far and wide along an open dirt path.
Each new step infuses its bones
With the fortitude of a carpenter's lath.

The eyes awaken. Hearts blossom near.
A faint voice beckons a song.
The mountains lift their veils, a stalk appears.
Rivers crest. We belong.

Home is where this tree now crops,
Where leaflets take flight on most days.
Where seeds kiss the brow of golden mountaintops,
While peace visits for a time, then stays.

Marcel Wormsley

Nocturne

Somewhere in the recesses of wayward thoughts
I approach the intersection where the
Cafe of Remembrances once stood.
I drink the last of its vestiges and
Beckon the street for a toast,
To ends and to beginnings and to the
Place where the nocturnes took repose
Just below voluptuous bosoms flush with
Smoke and light.

I Once Heard an Ode

I once heard an ode to the
Persistence of nimble dreams
Cavorting about as
Children along banks flush with white.
It said that the creek of daily sorrows
Had been frozen in time,
That its ripples had now crystallized into a
Colorful panoply of sagittate leaves all pointing in
Different directions, without destination,
Or with a view to all of them.

It said that magic no longer treads solely in the
Fertile garden of green minds,
But in little eyes scintillating with anticipation
And unconditional wonderment,
In homes warmed by the sustained flicker of
Sprightly, ruddy-faced harmonies,
In the way you peer out of the window to
Capture a distant gegenschein winking back at you,
Reminding you of that time when the
Impetuous laughter of innocence never had to knock.

It also said that a child is born
In all of us.
And then reborn.

Marcel Wormsley

In Search of Moonlit Crevices

Engulf Me, O Winter's Yawn

Engulf me, O winter's yawn
With your gleams of evanescent glory.
Immobilize me in your infinite knowing,
And tell me your story.

If you find me astray,
Bear me up with haste.
Reveal to me the end of self,
Through stones your precipitation graced.

Take me through endless mirrored corridors,
Where the howl of legends echoes each season.
Remember their fables when ages apart,
Until I find, in your breath, my reason.

Marcel Wormsley

Dear Time

What becomes of a fragile prelude that
Sounds in the distance along lunate
Arcs of scented fervor, like the lavender
Janus flower I plucked from the terrace of vain manifestos?

What becomes of the ravishing virtuoso maiden across the sea
Who channeled my affections in every note and stroke, where
No distance proved too great for passions duly united in
Art and song?

Of the long-lost father who never forgot my smile,
Of the community of gentle spirits who welcomed
My prodigal soul back home with tea and festive hearts?

Of the voice I re-discovered during a chance excursion
Into Chagallian dreamscapes, Munchain moonlit nights,
Van-Goghian pastures, Monetian sunrises along the creek
Of delicate remembrances?

What becomes of the consecration of words that
Flow from my hand into receptive worlds, where
Sentiments poured in earnest beautify and heal,
Illuminate and dissolve, reflect and portend?

What becomes of this leap into the depths of uncertain
Events, where shadows of days past are distilled into
Tiny little blueprints of full-blooded resolution?
Of action without reservation? Of change effected by
Mint-flavored frissons of existential clarity?

What will become of this prelude – and this flower—
As I toss them into this pond of expectations,
And the rings begin to flourish?

A Singular Movement

A singular movement,
Contained in a singular act,
Intoxicated by the savory liqueur of
Impassioned abductions of space,
Beckoned a new facet of her muted awareness,
Rendering an abundance of courteous attentions
In return for a singular glimpse of her
Retreat into the sanctum of a million disappearances.

Marcel Wormsley

Mistress of Emptiness

Mistress of emptiness,
Scented with lush uncertainty.
Tacit receptiveness,
Cloaked in subtle apathy.
Words unspoken are closer than they appear,
Lost sentiments closer still.

Embers slowly subside into
Walls dulled by shadowy gazes
Too tired to frolic to the
Pace of disjointed mazurkas.

The lips tremble slowly at the
Piquant savor of soft cherries
Saturated with the dense nectar of
Suppressed desire

(As they are wont to do)

Until what remains

Unsaid

Embalms
The hope of this, our final night of
Gratuitous liaison...
Don't weep until sunrise, love.
Preserve your honeyed silk for
Future embraces in another room,
In another world,
Where secrets will neither hear nor see.

II

As the Winds Subsist

As the winds subsist,
as the horizon broods,
a faint luminosity guides us along
ever-shifting and inconstant paths,
nocturnal awakenings and re-awakenings,
successive alignments across avenues
both well-worn and forgotten in time,
alien dream-like tableaux reified into
vaguely familiar vignettes of journeys past.

Marcel Wormsley

Teach Me

Teach me
Stillness.
Teach me
Primordial hope.
Teach me blindness
So that wayward eyes
Pierce the shrouds
Of everything that
Endures. Teach
My breath to become
As a wave turned
Upon itself as
It seeks confirmation
Through threshold-seeking
Tones of nascent glass.
Teach this light to
Speak the language of
The wayfarer's lament.
Digest its symbolism
And learn its journey
Through each new
Shade of meaning.
Teach the night
To believe again.

Thresholds

Thresholds of awareness
Exhumed from the abysmal flux
Of primordial being.
All that was infinitely
Forgotten
Now surrounds the
Temporal shield,
And penetrates it.

Marcel Wormsley

You Are Not Your Gaze

You are not your gaze.
Fate persists not
In the cupped, trembling hands
Of imaginary fools,
But in the seduction of eager flesh
Bound by endless tangled strands of
Liquefied reflection.

They Have Drunk

They have drunk from your decanter of sorrows.
Bathed in your iniquity.
What remains then of a tattered phantasm,
A consciousness vulnerable to the mind,
Yet vulgar to the eye?
Loneliness is a velvet cocoon,
Slowly ripped to fine shreds by the restless
Light of your virtue.

Marcel Wormsley

Rue Toulouse

Rue Toulouse was where I
Melded a dozen hopes
Into a waxen ball of
Panacea, wall-flower
Colored with veins
Engorged by steady currents
Of forgetfulness and the
Occasional colorless thought.

As the Seedling Goes

As the seedling goes,
So goes the wellspring of
Bounteous hopes;
Once a scant thought encapsulated
By the shell of uninterrupted possibilities,
A stalk solidifies and sheds its skin,
And images awaken from repose.
Tomorrow a garden bears her sundry fruits,
Hearkening to a season that flows through the lips
And to the center of every expectant heart.

Marcel Wormsley

Fortune Confronts a Shadow

Fortune confronts a shadow
Drunk with aberrant exultations
To instincts that dare to wonder.

Clarity is a majolica elephant flush with
Socratic thoughts and regrets;
But in time he awakens to grace
And lumbers quietly across
Electric pathways

Frozen in space.

Each Moment

Each moment brings me closer
To the delicate bounties that course
Along the of seams of her spirit,
Slowly lifting the nainsook lace veil
From her trembling visage.
She is new to this season,
But her tender fruit yields
In the stillness of courage.
I will sing her accolades until I lose myself
In the embryo of her lost time.

Marcel Wormsley

Groping Along

Groping along renascent bursts of pastoral virility,
Almost liquid now.
We can laugh soon enough,
And shake hands with the red-blooded lutenist
Just across the bank,
Just before the last note.

Falling Leaves

Autumnal tears of joy,
Whisked away by a faint zephyr
No less familiar to me
Than the one I knew
And surrendered to
In my youth;
That cooled my veins,
That caressed my budding heart,
That still whispers songs without words
On those days when I am all but
Convinced that the familiar melodies
Were never forgotten.

Marcel Wormsley

Fix My Movements

Fix my movements with your anxious glare.
Immobilize my arms in a labyrinth of
Soft, dewy tentacles
Engorged with a desire that chooses not to see.
Bind my feet with jesses of liquid lavender
As you trace meandering paths of pink taffeta
Across my undulating chest.
Move until my breath eludes me,
Until everything
Is alien.

Burgundy Nights

Her breath eludes me – it is alien.
Trembling hands glide restlessly
Through billowing burgundy satin dreams
So soft, so ethereal they slip from the hand
Like molten ruby.

I'm here, I'm not here.
I follow her, anxiously
Into a relentless density of wooded paths, united passions,
Curiosity ramified into infinite branches of intent.
Each one rising, falling

According to a smile – laughs, anticipations materialized.
She beckons me there. Deeper—
She's familiar with these worlds.
Already traveled, already there, waiting for the hand,
Or at least its shadow.

Aimless caresses ignite discrete flames,
Illuminating labyrinthine grottos decked with playful crevices
That glide, gently, hands interlocked,
Her eyes in repose, satin cries unraveled,
Gracing my countenance with delicate unrestraint.

I indulge her fury.
A small Death, all the sweeter,
Awakens latent streams flanked by the élan of
Reckless oblivion.
Within her bosom I am immersed in my cause
Without qualification,
Suffocated by the rapture of fleeting remembrances of
Those foreign nights.

Marcel Wormsley

In Search of Moonlit Crevices

How Might I Sound the Depths

How might I sound the depths
Of this unbridled verdure

That bursts forth unforeseen
From the silken grass
Along the edges of your watered eyes
Glimmering helplessly
Across a thousand lost Springs?

How might your light be multiplied
Among darkened ranges

Lush with uncertain hands
That glide conspicuously
Along the base of my neck,

Coming to rest upon my lips,
Where your name seeps in gently
Through drip after anonymous drip,
As I begin to recall
The path your melody took that one night
We planted emerald seeds
In the dust of our leftover dreams?

How might the intoxicating musk of feral roses
Enjoin me to dance

With the legerity of softened bones
Sweetened and subdued
By the candied spice
Abducted from your fulgurant whispers?

How might I digest our song
One last time

Until my heart overflows
With the rhythm
Of nocturnal Arabian masquerades,
And Eden uncloaks
And her naked silhouette
Beckons me to rest?

Marcel Wormsley

Intensive Introspection

Intensive introspection
Remained my weapon of choice
To parse and
Discreetly devour
Every component of a
Consciousness bloated to excess with
Rogue and wanton thought,
All while I continued to lust for that
Precise moment of redemption when
Immanence would happily dissolve into a
Vast decompression of
Uncooked, scintillating bits of hollow
Reflection impregnated by certainty.

The Lane

...Where one minute drifts forward,
The other behind me,
Another to my side.
They extend and retract,
Bending crosswise and releasing.
An infinity of them, perpetually shifting,
Reacting, building, weaving steadily
Along this well-worn path,
Searching for a beginning.

Marcel Wormsley

At the Barbershop

At the barbershop,
Where the exigencies of the day
Take a back seat to that long-anticipated
Urban interlude, wherein daily struggles
Are expounded in raw eloquence,
Intertwined with reflections of perennial fears,
Intermittent joys, and ever-fleeting souvenirs of purpose,
Where once a week Time can be seen walking by,
Entering inconspicuously, nodding, smiling,
Hanging his fedora on the rack while discarding his
wristwatch.

Light Speaks Our Language Tonight

Light speaks our language tonight,
Dutifully approximating some kind of love.
Not just evanescent impressions of infatuated glares
Buried in moments of vaunted soliloquy,
But a luminous passion that wanders and gathers about
Seeking embodiment, then returns again
By the crest of nightfall to its rightful place
In every bosom that awaits
With bated anticipation of some kind of glory
Found drifting along gently inflamed waters
Bearing restless reflections that frolic and flicker
In their own time,
Yet always just in time to capture a few errant kisses
Carefully-worded
With silent inhibitions to rest.

Marcel Wormsley

Sultana of the Sun
(For Woman)

Sultana of the Sun,
Light your candles.
Hold them against your earthly casting
Until it awakens and begins to melt.

Watch it as it seeps into current,
Separating, coalescing, separating anew.
What is the color of a waxen womb
That sculpts and molds
Its own exodus toward atonement?

Feel your awareness blossom into
A procession of softened flesh
Coruscating with the abandoned sway
Of particles infused with
Harmonies perpetually reborn.

Move with them through darkened moons
And pristine, sunswept capes.
Nurture them as the dust that
Scurries along each moistened strand
Of your sea-silken hair,
Seeking refuge upon the tender peaks of
Saturated breasts.

Mind the brittle bones of rhythms immemorial.
Find your ghosts and careen with them.
Render supplication with coffrets bearing
Lubricious gazes and oblique steps
Toward dimensionless borders.

Unearth the wings you once buried in shame.
Scream until your voice coincides
With the transcendent cry of the original drifting Womb.
Meet me where the current ends
And we'll enter it together,
And bathe in its igneous expulsion.

In Search of Moonlit Crevices

If you are tired you can rest here
Upon this tuft of sand.
And tomorrow you can fly
Back through the tunnels your graceful reveries have fashioned,
Back into the arms of a lotus you once knew,
Planted while you were asleep
By a spry and expectant Dawn.

Marcel Wormsley

Look Away

Look away,
And in time you will see them.
They persist
As little droplets of unrequited passion,
Given to merciful hands
That excise all relation to thought.
In this moment
Allow your truth to reveal its scars;
Let them dry and close up.
Let them cry at will.
Let them stare back at you
Until you are moved
And incapacitated.
There is no wind here to carry you.
There are no shadows to cajole you.
Run, then sleep.
If you awaken early, run again.
Forget your futures.
Burrow jagged paths
That radiate from those barren pastures
Where your heart used to be.
Face them on all sides
And explore each
With diligence and abandon.
In time you will be startled by a whisper.
They will have remembered your name.
And you will look back,
And you will see them.

I Am a Child

I am a child
Of hands apart.
I sway to scattered muses
Tethered to reluctant arms.
I scamper down rubato paths
Lined with fine green mist
And twisted blades
Of fibreless grass.
I have a meeting
With the elders of open worlds
And free-roaming beginnings.
I will reunite with friends
And sing them my joys.
What lies beyond this towering hillside
I may never know,
Or want to know.

Marcel Wormsley

There Are Many Mirrors Here

There are many mirrors here,
But none so translucent
As the one I turned away from
Moons and stars and galaxies ago,
When your possibility entered my awareness

And the dark corners that dutifully inhabit your space
Culminated into many precipices,
Each one beckoning me to leap
Into this sea that churns with unknowing-
Head unbowed, arms outstretched, hands trembling

As I clutch this mirror tightly; yes, the one I made for you,
Moons and stars and galaxies ago,
Now cracked in many places and blurred by the constant gale of
Moments perpetually come and gone
In this happy continuum of

Nothingness and light.
Before I take flight, it must be shattered
And cast into the sea,
And each piece will bear the faintest of illuminations
Until fully dissolved.

I will latch on to one,
And let it guide me home
Until it too becomes another moment,
Another memory weaved into
This vast wreath of possibilities both already realized and yet to be.

If I arrive not,
Remember not my failed journey,
But cherish the light that became its beginning,
And connect it with others
Until the circle is complete.

Here

Here,
Cosmic distances
Have kissed their limits
Hello and goodbye.
And 'ere the moment
They are at last embowered
By these watchful arms
A keeper emerges in the offing
Without a word,
Speaking only with compassionate hands
That toil ceaselessly in iridescent shadows
Cast by a remote awareness
Of where the smallest path once lay bare,
Dutifully awaiting a chance at perfection.

Marcel Wormsley

Water

Startled by the shrill cries of feathered sable-winged imps, I awaken.

I stumble with purpose to the bathroom, turn on the faucet, allowing the stark cold deluge of life to overtop my cupped hands. Perched over the sink like a sordid mendicant in the throes of his final prostration, I am momentarily transfixed by the effortless and inconstant swishing and swirling, movement upon movement, all manner of transparent, tenuous being turning back on itself.

Just as soon as it is there, it is not, and no sooner it is there again. In a singular thrust my face is fully immersed, arising to a glass bespattered with errant streams scurrying toward the white porcelain base like fugitive tears from a dozen eyes, giving it a cracked and mottled appearance. I am confronted by a mere semblance of a man, slipping in and out of definition, his visage melting and separating into disjointed components of an indifferent and superfluous reality.

I peer out of the kitchen window, expecting to find the imps alighting on the balcony's ledge. They usually gather around at this time to discuss the day's events, to celebrate the passing whispers of days and seasons, to plan, plot, make love, then polish their sleek swept-back wings for yet another excursion.

They are gone. Treeless limbs rest lethargically in the distance, valgus and brittle. The rays of a rapidly descending sun cast them in a particularly stark and reprehensible relief. I make my way to the door, turning back once to take in this vast expanse of muddled ambitions. For the first time I leave it unlocked. A clear, bitter calipash congeals around my neck, through my nose, and over my eyes no sooner than I can manage two steps outside, asphyxiating me whole with stoic hands that only toil in withered fields.

I push my way past a gaggle of unkempt urchins frolicking aimlessly along the side street that eventually leads up to the old abandoned tea house two or so blocks east. I make my way south down towards the sparsely-dressed hillock that seems to be in perpetual solicitation for souls or at least a once-in-a-year ablution from the fleeting but curious clouds.

To my right is the road to Happy Ville where I often drowned myself in liquid sanity and floated along swells of lusty, sweltering bacchants with no faces. A particularly fearsome bacchante bedecked in an exotic suite of blue nainsook, rose beads and flowers coruscates with vulgar abandon, cheered on enthusiastically by bearded virtuoso vagabonds camped on the corner with whatever managed to produce just enough euphonious strands of harmony to get them through another night.

Two knights perched on horses look on with authority half subdued by prurient amusement. Tonight I drift along implacable currents of beings who knew no care but their own, bodiless heads weaving in and out of art galleries and watering holes like little organic molecules connected by skeins of dilapidated spirits and proud destitution. For all the activity, there is no life in this place.

I stand atop the hillock and set my gaze on the lake below, coloring it with what little my eyes have left. Forms arise, disappear, then back again, but always stagnant, an enticing tableau vivant bedewing my affections with delicate but devilish hands. My form is incomplete, my body a disjointed mass turning back on itself to find completion in a broken world. "It's all vain, vain," I cry, wringing my sweaty hands as I ponder the depths for all the answers I've ever needed.

Marcel Wormsley

In Search of Moonlit Crevices

Honor

Honor is a tussock of pliant grass
That bows in unison
To the call of a plower's chant.
Regal are the trees
That guard the gates of seven horizons,
Each one in timeless repose
While his neighbor is awakened.
A kingdom is summoned here;
Of bodies through portals
Of transcendent humility,
Of breezes that mark the hour
Of seven stages of reckoning,
Of a glorious perspective
That sways in concert
With the hands of the gods.

Marcel Wormsley

Flash of the Crow

These eyes have laid bare
A tendency to drift
Among currents of
Impalpable impressions of thought,
Wherein only the wither'd vestiges
Of youthful wings doth abound,
Now intermittently aflutter
To the last plainchant of the grave warden
Resolutely resigned to his own extinction:

A solitary wind meanders on,
Too noble for stagnation,
But too humble for forgiveness.
Every color is uprooted and scattered
Along this serpentine path,
Until usurped by velvety drops of blackened rain
That slowly fill a wooden ladle
Perched against a desiccant rock
That patiently abides a child's return.

She once kept post at the entrance
To a vale of wonderment-
Unconditionally-
Where the cackle of children
Flourished day and night, freely conceived
Amid raucous cavalcades
Of homespun instruments,
Where artless impromptu anthems
Blared possibilities that became harmony
And harmony recalled
Colorful vignettes
Of its own possibility
During occasions of tenderness.

From time to time
The winds would heed
Her strident call to order.
And a cluster of buds
Would dance their Christening dance
As the flocks looked on
With amusement.
These were the times
Her silken essence
Glistened the most,
Reflecting restless, variegated hues
Perpetually seeking flight
Back into the womb of the Sun.

One day she left,
No sooner than she appeared.
The children are now asleep,
Hastened to rest
By an unbidden hiatus in verse.
All that is left to wonderment
Is absorbed in a sodden chimera
Of beady unblinked eyes
And a violent twitch
Of a deciduous patchwork coat
That glistens no more.

From this abandoned ladle
Harmony takes a drink
And begins to remember
A song from old,
But the words escape him.

Marcel Wormsley

Growth Happens When

Growth happens when
Many shadows collide at once,
And the air begins to quiver;
When the fifth Sun arises
From his slumber
And makes sweet love to
A distant ocean;

When somewhere along the periphery
Of these jagged cliffs
A bishop lies in the sand,
Smiling and remembering,
And chanting to the seagulls;

When I happened upon
A weather-worn seashell
Bearing exotic fruits,
And I palpated her seductive edges,
But did not eat;

When the webbed gossamer
Donned a spare petticoat
And began to fly,
'Ere the moment I decided
To pray for the first and last time;

When I suffocated myself
In this coarse, directionless frock
In whose skin you might find
Some of the eternal answers
And the questions that impregnated them;

When I came home to a striking array
Of pastel-colored houses with no windows,
Overgrown gardens with no flowers,
And sinuous dusty streets
Endlessly teeming with decrepit cafes
Emanating sounds of droll laughter
From patrons with no bodies;

In Search of Moonlit Crevices

When I severed my heart,
Dividing it equally into
A thousand twitching little pieces,
And fed them to the pigeons,
When the edifice of faith
Reduces to rubble,
And the vestiges of piety
Abandon their shrines:
Blessed is the winged flame
That rises and engulfs
The overgrown structures
Of passive thoughts.

Marcel Wormsley

Light: An Elegy

A light shimmers in the fore,
Joined by the hand
Of song and rhythm
And lambent dances
Along a moonlit creek in repose.

What does it see
Beyond this specter
Of jaded spirits
And world-weary migrations
To parts hitherto untold
That beckons its uncompromising smile?

From whence does its melody arise
That it traverses so calmly
Through dimensions and landscapes
Hitherto unseen?

When will a world
Left in silent agony
Learn its dance
And free itself from
These windless vales
Of stagnant tears?

A light begins to fade in the offing,
Just beyond the directionless bend.
As she retracts her hand
To commence one more excursion

She speaks,

Gently reminding the creek
That upon her return,
A new song will be sung,
And a new rhythm mapped out
For posterity.

In Search of Moonlit Crevices

And the shiftless vale will blossom
With a chorus of sparrows
And flora bedecked with purple amaranths
Heralding a new day,
In which smiles are freely-given
And hearts are open
For the weary traveler
To stop and rest awhile,
Before the next journey.

Marcel Wormsley

Shattered Melodies

Shattered melodies
Beget gems aglimmer
With innocent wonder.
When Finality sings
Her impatient aria
Every gem returns
To alignment
And all is forgiven.

Deep in the Vagaries

Deep in the vagaries
Of blind thought
A sentinel emerges
And waits for the call of
Blue laughter and
Pain covered with restless ivy.

Land and sea are one,
The clouds have fallen
Into disrepute, and
A once sprightly zephyr
Has become embittered
By the relentless dogmatism
Of snowy mirages
Barely frozen.

Marcel Wormsley

Rhythm

Rhythm: flowing through,
And flooding over,
Exuding power,
And keen to purpose;
Committing to
Hand and foot,
Indulging
The laborer's sweat to
Oblivious intoxication.
But awakens
Posthumously,
And hastily embraces
An abandoned shovel.

Run from Truth

Run from truth.
Penetrate uncertainty
With equal measure
Of fear and trembling.
These sultry springs want to listen;
Typically, they are the last to be forsaken.
Enter into the chalice of abandoned wonderment
And cast this broken flower amid the ruins.

You will remember the limp crow
That strained to bid you goodnight,
And the brief turbulence
That gave multiple births
To illusions of villages
Unaware of the frowning circle
Patiently waiting to devour them.

And digest them,
Whole,
Until each villager turns in upon himself,
And cowers in desolation.
His heart will be there for the borrowing,
For lusty hands to fill
A hatchet-shaped hole in the ventricle,
That it may smile again,
Restlessly perhaps.

Truth sits in a wretched dacha
Just beyond this darkness,
Sipping on lukewarm tea
Punctuated with sweet bits of brimstone.

A black feather courses in the window,
Searching for nothing.
A piece of leafless stalk binds it from the rear,
And keeps it from blowing away
For now.

Marcel Wormsley

The Arms of Safekeeping

The arms of safekeeping
Strengthened with each casting
Of the twilight bell.
Gracious and swift
Do they mark each row
Where increments of time
Retract and spread
In imperfect unison,
Like disengaged atoms
Along errant waves.

When the moment becomes you,
Travel lightly along the
Sand-soaked precipice,
And smell the dreams as they
Strive to appear
Without warrant,
But with fullness
Of meaning found buried
Beneath the withered castles
You have created for me.

Bells
(after Picasso's Guernica)

Bells.
Glass.
Dust.
Water.
Arms.
Piety.
Yearning.
Screams.
Breathlessness.
Torn mandylions.

Flight.
Remission.
Redemption.
Combustion.
Blindness.
Doubt.
Divination.
Prayers.
Unleavened hearts.

Flowers.
Deadwood.
Delirium.
Red.
Oration.
Flares.
Bones.
Flightless birds.

Advancement.
Requiem.
Claws.
Cracks.
Rust.
Undercroft.
Consecration.
Sanguiferous sarabande.

Marcel Wormsley

Farruca.
Parasites.
Nihilism.
Clouds.
Quellios.
Suffocation.
Twists.
Whips.
Daggers.
Jagged boleros.

Sweat.
Cold.
Dusk.
Smoke.
Grey.
Silence.

Reluctant sunrise.
Broken Stones.

In Search of Moonlit Crevices

White Stone

A white stone tumbles slowly
Along a deserted beachside
While a fair mist takes flight in the distance,
Carrying with it spirited melodies
And conversations that drew circles
On walls eroded by legions of
Chapped hands grasping at
A frayed baton perpetually in retreat.

Here, a star is planted on fertile ground
And watered with the blood
Of youthful impetus and memories of home
Become remote as the gentle crow
Perched atop a lonely buoy
Prostrate in eternal supplication.

It shrieks in tune to a mother's last kiss
And remembers all the lullabies not sung
But not yet forgotten,
Or all the blemished letters
Jumbled in safekeeping,
Including the one with the words "home soon"
On the bottom,
Readable to only the most restive eyes.

A name emerges indistinctly
On an edifice of wandering souls
Awaiting muster's call.
What life does it embody,
Save a faceless history
Of unanswered calls for a
Surrender of bad faith
To conscience and humanity?

Where does each point of this star meet
In a unity of final purpose,
Where the shore engulfs the last stone
And retreats to a place where Glory
Disrobes her dubious sateen cloth?

Marcel Wormsley

Where a comrade is here to greet
A fellow survivor for the last time,
Before one of them enters the depths
Of remembered feats
Relegated to motionless distances?

The souls have gathered up
And they spring forth as the
Children they had begun to love
And continue to, stronger still.
Look at these hands,
And count the scars,
But also count the impressions
Of multifarious seeds that blossom
In remembrance of these walls,

These dedicated parchments
Fortified by the chapped skin
Of hands that dared not cease

Reaching forth,

And grabbing,

Finding,

And reliving.

The Fattened Swards

The fattened swards have
Met their limits,
And now mingle with
Rotating earthen bodies
That puff and flex
Across unknowable distances,
Yielding habitations erected by
A guilty love of baked cornmeal
Most nights by the fire below.

Tranquility is no more
Stable than the most
Disconnected thatchwork region
That squirms and writhes
With every compression
From above;
Opening,
Closing,
Blossoming,
Shriveling,
Anew.

Marcel Wormsley

A Tuft of Brisk Air

A tuft of brisk air,
Unglued and pressed
In every direction;
Kneaded across this lonely slate
With naive paws
Given to groping about
These dampened walls
With nary a method or skill.
And lo, the guards have taken post,
And have presided over forms
That seldom change
But resist transfixion.
Breathe with silent flames
And this slate comes alive,
And becomes your home again.

Heeding the Veiled Call

Heeding the veiled call of the sea
Whereupon elements of
Intermittent truths abound,
We pushed with the borrowed fortitude
Of hallowed and transient awareness,
Segmented by traces of a moon's swift touch.

We hunted the winds and quartered them,
Dutifully placing them at the edges of
Our darkened peripheries,
Marking an approximate end
To every course we
Had ever hoped to surmount.

With irregular bursts of passion
We ignited flares to
Illuminate the history of
Many a journey lost,
Only to dissipate back into
Hazy embarkations,
Blurred shorelines
And muffled soundings.

Marcel Wormsley

Abduct My Prayer

Abduct my prayer
From this place.
Tear this drabbet sackcloth
With the pineal thorns
Of your forgotten regard
For my ashen essence.

Expose me for the birds
To gather and pollinate
And render ablution
To these fossilized arms
Until they begin to retract
(For all time).

Study these hands and divine a place
Where nothing is fully known
Unless I rise nightly
With the ghosts
Of this well-mourn'd spot
And shuffle with them fluently.

Innocence Has Returned (Briefly)

Innocence has returned briefly
To gather his loose ends
And then off to the next
Excursion.

Perhaps whereupon his subsequent return
He may find that the borders
Have been compressed and smoothed out,
But still glistening under scarcely-palpable
Zephyrs and perpetually unraveling
Seams of disconnected light.

That will be the day when
The rivers drown themselves in forgetfulness
While the poppy fields look on
In amusement, shame,
Or a mixture of both.

Marcel Wormsley

I Know Well

I know well
That
I shouldn't want you.
I stifle
Desire and care
With all the fury
Of a corrupted saint
Entreating moments
Past and future for mercy.
And atonement.

I know that
Spirits are astir
Within me
With vague intentions.
A specter of desire
Comes to rest
On the ridge of your vein
Where your palm begins
To stroke my face.
Three phantasmal
Little urchins
Dally precariously
With the threshold
Of my awareness
Of your presence,
Threatening to obscure it
With three shades of dust
In the name
Of perpetual penitence,
Of chaste lullabies
Forcing rest.

I know well
That
You do not see me.
You have never seen me
And never will
Save through chipped glass
Thickened with
Red wine turned to gel
Encrusted with
Unanswered appeals
To tomorrow,
Using the songs of old.
But with your voice
Clarity arises
And makes the flute cry
(Like yesterday),
Perhaps at the sight
Of empty crystalline
Sparrows
All gathered along
The river bend
Where I shall want to
Accompany you,
Tomorrow.

Marcel Wormsley

A Stillness Suffices for the Moment

A stillness suffices for the moment
While I rescind all restraint.
Faint persuasions are moved to the back of my throat
Allowing me to divine paths
Of supple remembrances
With residual breath.

I weep as the lowly violin excretes
A labdanum of succulent grace unsought
That trickles down the painted sleeves
Of a golden horse's caftan
Circling its trembling leg
As a new healing heralds
A remorseless search
For justification.

It won't reach the floor
But will daily emerge at the edge, and dry up.
And the will to believe will linger
On a thickened tongue
Unable to move.
I may sojourn here
Without so much as a sip,
While the horse falls asleep.

When the violin shutters,
Say nothing,
But feel the anointment
Gracing its head.
Then course the unctuous string
With gentle fingers
Until you feel the impression
Of a distant pulse.

Three Hourglasses

Three hourglasses
Stand side by side
Each filled with coarse black sand.

Peering silently
Into distances without aim
Or countenance,
They have accepted
That fury is dead,
That the gilded raven
Still cries for remission
From remnants of shivering liturgies
Robbed of their skin.

Reflection has eaten itself raw
Into a vast burrow
With bores on every side
Slithering caterpillar-like into
A destiny of hollow regrets
And tawdry labyrinthine eulogies.

A crack emerges and spreads
Like a self-directed pestilence
Amid a population of
Scattering anti-heroes
And descending demi-gods.

Dust forms along the base of
Dreams that have long dissipated
Into an infinity of somber particulars.
Future accompanies a hapless paradise
Into a darkened chamber
Filled with breathless beady-eyed imps
Panting out old southern hymns
From their soot-drenched songbooks.

Marcel Wormsley

What the coming rain fails to redeem
We will want to keep embalmed
In this container
However imperfect;
However damaged,
Until the shell is ready to be
Compromised,
And the demons let out,
One, by one, by one.

A Feather Drifts in the Offing

A feather drifts in the offing
While new horizons are wedded
To teal dreams that age gracefully
Along wistful paths that
Will some day
Pray
To have re-entered
The womb of
Born-again desires
In order
To breathe
Anew, so that
Silken stars are
Carefully placed
Along blinded trellises
That knew horizons few,
But which laughter
Promptly illumined
And curiosity
Quickly forgot.

Marcel Wormsley

Black Rain

Black rain,
Thy redemption hearkens near.
Through withered toils
And misbegotten beginnings
Thy promise of absolution
Will soon set upon
These wasted fruits,
And carry them to grace.

Unguided Howls

Unguided howls
Unsteady drift;
Splashes of
Dusky gray
Overcome
By intermittent
Darkness;
In due moments
Passions will be swept
Heedlessly back to their
Distant forebears
Where primordial
Forgetfulness
Awaits
Unglued
And a final reckoning of
Every muster brought
To account.
The sun may rise
But its rays will be blue
Just in time for devotion.

Marcel Wormsley

Free Yourself

Free yourself
From the moment,
Then digest it.
Do not chew it,
But let it disintegrate
At its own pace
And nourish you
And cause you to tingle
With feral nymphs
Each beckoning you to
Scream
While the pangs
Of your ecstasy
Or fury
Or desire
Find their voice.
Another moment will come,
But do not eat it.
Let it linger at the
Fringes of your lips
Until it implodes
Through too many pointed
Frissons of
JOY
Each pushing against the skin
In search of words to steal
And a song or two
To keep them aloft.

Down at the Alameda

Down at the alameda
We shook hands,
Laughed,
Told stories,
Then laughed some more,
Until we forgot.

It was the place
Where life happened unconditionally,
Where leaves found their rhythm
In errant breezes
And paused to collect
A tear or two;

Where I once found a shell
With ridges decayed
Punctured with a tinge of lust
That tickled the jaws
Of feral plum seeds
Stripped of their memories
And spewed forth
From the mouths of happy beasts.

Marcel Wormsley

And Then There Came

And then there came
The remembrance of her gaze,
And how it once blossomed into
A panoply of flames
Enveloping strands of night
That had begun to
Creep and settle
As fine dust
Along the estuary

Where our desires
Took rest in the other's arms
But dared not dream,
Lest they give rise to
Fallen motifs and familiar whispers
And faded letters penned
During Falstaffian winters

When your affection
Diligently counted the ashes
That was once my heart
And scattered them,
Speck by speck,
Into waters that never knew passion.

But oh, upon this maiden's hand
Do I commend
This decaying memory
Of restless brushes along my arm
And gentle bouts of laughter
'Neath the trellis
At water's end;

Of her glow that writes
Well into the night
Tracing the spheres
As they dare to appear.

In Search of Moonlit Crevices

That Morning

That morning,
Not a ripple remained among us
That did not encompass some thought
About yesterday.

We endeavor to keep them all,
And feast with them,
Inspecting them for clarity
Of hindsight and reflection.

They have kissed the breeze
Of their own accord,
And have delighted in their secrets,
Half-divulged,
In concert with vague movements.

They tell us nothing,
But show us what it means
To be the salvation
That awaits them
With a half-smile

One night
Years ago.

Marcel Wormsley

Feel

In free form
A raindrop wanders.
Your buds unraveled
Springtime.

A tuft of hair
Glides restlessly along
An undulating chest
Blue taffeta
Tethered to your wrist
Gently tightened.

The shift is complete.
Emotions have been shuffled
Like spry billiard balls.
There is no solace here;
Just attempts to feel
And exhaustion
In the feeling.

Fleeting breaths
Pulsating bosom adrift
Silent corners.

Nervous hands clasped
Unto the jagged breasts of
Salvation,
But palpates nothing.
I think,
And I am not.

Little gnomes are aflutter, naked,
And taunt the flightless beasts
Who saunter along
Pasturages unforgiving.

What does it mean
To cry or want to cry
When the spirit remains
Immobile,
Having exchanged its incandescence
For intermittent songs
Of dusk and smoke?

When a soiled fist emerges from the ground
Scarred by his only savior?
When a new day dawns and
A gnome's wing is shorn
And divided into equal portions
For beast and serpent alike,
And the flightless gnome
Begins to wonder, and worry

Until the hand begins to bloom
And a ladle carrying my porous heart
Is placed within reach
Until your return?

Fill it with your hollow tears
If you must.
Drown it in all matter of
Sublime remembrance
Of a sun that wades along the precipice
In search of a reason
To console this grounded wretch
Back to flight.

Devour the thorned rose of guilt
Slowly.
Recall the dance of the mountaintops
When their skin began to peel on all sides
Revealing compacted stacks of
White heat, smooth and deadly to the touch,
But enough to feel again,
And become.

Marcel Wormsley

In Search of Moonlit Crevices

Piece by Piece

Piece by piece
Our journey realigned itself
In concert with
Sprightly reassurances
From across a budding millpond,

Enjoining us to sing
When there is no breath,
To kiss with lips gilded by
The dew of daysprings past,
To love beyond the last heartbeat.

Moment by moment
Our paths would sound
The hollow depths of beginnings
Reborn with the scent of meadow's musk

And take rest together
Where the pebbles begin to glisten
One face-down, the other face-up,
Without a blink,
Until the firmament beckons the stone
And the stone smiles in return.

Marcel Wormsley

Expand Undefined

Expand undefined
Until these brittle forms

Leave no
Trace of
Original grasp.

Contract when
Light gives you
Every reason to
Suffer and
Not to see.

Invert your sorrows
Upend every regret
So that you die only once,
Knowing.

Where We Are Going

Where we are going,
Enigmas await
With hands extended
Bearing ripe stones,
Expressionless cabochon
Droplets of stilted rain,
Or a petty curse from
The fountains below.
Beyond this threshold
You are masked,
Surrounded by ever-advancing
Entrails of an abandoned Spring.
Without movement
You've become an efflorescent statue
Mocking time and
Pilfering its colors
Until the last one is drawn
Patiently and elegantly devoured,
Just in time for the advent
Of the weakened penumbra
You freed years ago one morning
Blanketless now in the cool of dusk,
Naked, with trembling feet
Smiling tentatively.

Marcel Wormsley

I Knew You Were There

I knew you were there.
I dreamt it
One night
By the fireside
Of your bounteous imagination.

Your hands
Only told me so much
When wrapped tightly
Around my shell of inconstancy,

When it breaks
I will be there to recover the pieces
And I will peer into them
And follow every ridge to the end of space.

I knew you were not
Before they noticed.
Your song was hastened
And in vast disarray.

You never finished
But I was there to applaud you
And walk you to the pond
Where you vowed to
Cast your restless ghosts.

Your scarlet armure coat
Lies here on my bed
Still dusty from the last excursion
And missing a button.

I wrap myself in it sometimes
And pretend it's my shell.
You incubate me,
And I am blind to all except
Your whimsical patterns
And the acrid, smoke-twilled
Scent that follows them.

In Search of Moonlit Crevices

I knew you were with me
When my body became still
And faced consecration
To the dusty ages
Where Time refused to go.

We reflected on the rise of
An abandoned moon
Coruscating with desire in all directions;
It would be our new home,
The place where you would

Come to rest
After journey's end,
And before I awaken you,
I will consolidate your thoughts
Into elongated spheres
Of approximate histories
And gauzy projections
Of future tidings,

As we dance arm in arm
To the beginning of certainty,
Where I will have been
Already awaiting your return,
Coat in hand.

Marcel Wormsley

Be Still

Be still
And revere in solitude
A bosom above
That awaits us.

Soon we will engorge it
With a patient eye that
Traverses the mornings
In blissful repose
Sliding along rapacious
Tongues that could never
Withstand emptiness.

Suffice it for the moment
That they be one and all
Put to rest by the artless
Smile of the naked sapling
Who dances in remembrance
Of naught but the warm
Hand that guides her

And feeds her fig leaves
In the mists of noonday.
Pray to the elongated breast
That coils around the tree branch
Of certitude and warmth,
Slithering its way to the ground
Where the extra leaves have gone to wither.

Nourishment is here!
Joy is here!
Long live the setting of your arms
Across my chest
Whenever the sun forgets!

Come to my abode and
Adorn it with blue stones,
Remember when my wings
Begin to blossom again
And hearken it to the kingdom
At hand.

Your lips will sing the praises of
Trails that fought against being lost
And your other hand; yes, that one, will keep
The angels afloat,
Lest their feet become heavy
And their wings brittle
With forgotten time.

Marcel Wormsley

In Search of Moonlit Crevices

Briefly

Briefly
Things take shape
Then disappear.
When the eye blinks,
The reverie is dead
And new light becomes
The angel in you
For a time,
Then you are whisked away
By gratuitous moments
Undefined and barely in view.
When I think of crying,
Something awakens
And you are there,
Listening, breathing,
A simple melody
Exhorting me to rest
Before you arrive again
And I extend my hands
To greet you
Wordless.

Marcel Wormsley

Faithfully

Faithfully,
The impression of your hand in mine
Lingers in a pool of usurped moments
As I cast my shadow down the hill
Where I coveted your face
With searching lips
For the first and last time.
The centuries will hear me beseech
And expand as tunnels inundated with the
Dust of the beloved and the fallen.
The ferns will outgrow their bodies
And begin to sashay nimbly above the
Moon-glazed swards that birthed them.

Gratuitously,
The tortoise will remember to smile again,
And his legs will gain strength
As his journey decompresses
And his resting place arises in a gale of
Furious, breathy arias
Abiding their impending freedom.
Should the seas open up for your arrival
And your star begins to weep,
Do not wait for me,
For timeless I have become.
We have loved as the tiller's dream
Loved the hillside,
As the edifice now loves its song.

Uncharacteristically,
You might find me buried deep in the trough
With mirrors on all sides.
Do not seek my likeness,
For I am all of them
And probably none of them.

Fear nothing as you close your eyes
And slowly restrain your breath.
Do not awaken until infinity has
Called you to behold two smiling trees in the fore.
Open your eyes,
Go lie among them,
Eyes facing the sea,
And breathe again,
Just a little at a time.

Marcel Wormsley

Bereft of Words
(Service and Protection)

Bereft of words,
Save for this small exhortation I found
Lying in the middle of the street.
It wanted desperately for me to help him
Find his face, or something fairly close to it,
So that he could finally be seen again,
And perhaps even interacted with;
As x approaches the (a) limit of civility.

Afterwards we would locate his jar of coagulated thoughts
And loosen them with his mother's tears,
The vagrant shadows of possibilities
Forever unrealized lurking restlessly
Within the hollowed-out space of each anguished drop.

Nevermind the blood that cascades from his chest;
Its song will end soon enough,
And you will be forced to interpolate its lyrics
Between each panged session, each rupture
Of salvation from clot after blessed clot.

Churning and churning,
A fire persists with
Each successive wave growing more robust than the last
In a furor of abandon withstood only by an escaping sun.
There is no life in this place,
Because he remained invisible
Up to the moment the eyes of the other
Encapsulated him whole
Before the first words could take form.

Solace the hearts as you may,
But you will not find him
In your good will.
Your fear is where they have made his home;

In Search of Moonlit Crevices

Where you defend against him, daily,
Pushing him into the throes of immobility
And depersonalization as you
Seek refuge from all that
Dare mention his name.

In the end, though,
He is but waiting to be born.
You will see him.
And he will know a pure sun.

Marcel Wormsley

The Way Your Eyes Twitch

The way your eyes twitch

In the candlelight
Does not lie.
A million wonders
And I find you here among
A shadow that prays
For penitence,
A million more ways to sunset.

Kiss me at once,
Mold my being with your
Questionless lips.
Deny not the ghosts of
Preludes past entrance between us.
Let them bloom violently
Until the passion subsides
With the morning seaside
Upon its return home.

War boasts not only for the wicked,
But for the plainsong of the lustful and the restless
Who fight for the tattered shawl that
Love left tied to the rock below,
The one we once thought was immovable
But that now appears to drift a little.

Silent Inhibitions to Rest
(Meditations on Aloneness)

I am stillness,

Beholding the innocuous gesture of a
Recurrent and timely presence.
It encompasses me whole,
Embracing me with a dire earnestness and constancy of grasp,
A veritable representation
Of an old man's impetuous but fleeting importunacy
for an unattainable
Survival and redemption.
But is it I alone whom Nature herself has perchance decreed
To succumb so readily unto this damp, caliginous mass of apathy,
Habited in its old familiar accouterments,
Bespeaking the eternal languor and quietude its hand imports?
Nary a sound...a single utterance even.
Very well, but if it is indeed the case that I stand so decreed,
Then for what purpose, what cause?
Obligation screams from within, but I cannot be so moved.
It becomes but a feckless and stifled show of potential and ideal
I cannot attend.

I cannot return her embrace,

And must wonder whether in good faith this gesture really be.
I stand blindfolded, an adynamic blob of unrequited existence
With hushed breath.
In my last efflux my independence is proclaimed
And I am surely bereft of him
For good,
Knowing him only in the evanescence of disconnected globules
which
Fall
From the
Precipice in pure
Freedom.

I am constricted.

Marcel Wormsley

Brooding arms, warm and callous; a distinct heaviness in the breast
That obtrudes, enjoining me to palpate a blunt lump of discarded soul,
Which startles me. My subjugation awaits.
Perhaps it is on a quest of sorts, a movement of insatiable pursuit to
Breach the sanctum sanctorum of all my life's energies and
Protective tendencies.
All efforts at resistance fail, all new passions aborted.
All creative inspirations, self-preserving propensities, nascent and past,
Presently bound unto this sad, sprawling vale of shiftless moments and
Privation for its own sake.

I am oppressed.

A salient fury it has not, like the e'er so rapacious flame that
Traipses about in search of men who will feed his familiar hauteur with
Forced awe, vaunting of his imminent identification
With a consummate and definitive
Destruction, masquerading convincing airs of nobility.
A comportment far more passive, but no less devious
Informs his every move and
Impresses upon me a stark-naked indifference,
Uncompromising, unconditioned in effect.
Surely if I am to be consoled by this latent innocence
I could never hope to more clearly perceive,
Then why do I stand here helpless, with roving arms, fleshless hands,
Enveloped in merciless vulnerability?
It oft vexes me the degree to which this thing contents itself
On being such a relentless
Self-perpetuation of mutually-sustaining contrasts,
A paradox of unified and complementary expressions
Of euphony and cacophony,
Of coarse black sand stuffed into hourglasses,
But whose flow knew no beginning.
It happily abounds in the very dearth it encapsulates,
A taste doubtless bitter to
Discriminating tongues.
But verily even in this bitterness a certain sweetness emerges,
Manifesting sections of its hitherto concealed face through
Spasmodic implosions of youthful vitality.

It abides. It moves.

In Search of Moonlit Crevices

It traverses worlds, minds.
With a peculiar yet seemingly characteristic élan
It commences its solidification into a
Confounding and omnivorous quintessence of intricate paths
Which I am forced to follow without the ability or
The wherewithal to render it
Meaning or purpose.
I question its intent. I question mine.
Why does ambivalence cry forth so steadily,
Blurred by a million droplets of shame?
Perchance it is I who embodies this ambivalence as such.

I am perplexed beyond all meaning, purpose, or intent.

Do I seek to be uplifted, nurtured, forever ravished
By this fathomless mass of being
One and all at rest, signified only
By this dense effluvium that lingers about,
Usurping that original purity and fluidity of breath
I once so intimately knew?
Or is my heart but a positive catalyst for an unwarranted sorrow,
For tears freely tendered, tenuously grasped, and eternally lost?
One certainty remains:
there is no escaping the ubiquity of freely roving
Monsters of solitude,
For their existence is neither dependent
On the transient humanity it affects,
Nor upon the transient affections of humanity.

It saturates. It defines.

It stands as the ultimate limit of my inception,
And the very terminus of all my dear life's possibilities
borne therefrom.
It is my b*eginning an*d my end.
Inasmuch as I am blindly abhorrent of it
I am helplessly enslaved by it.
There is no pride in my fall.
My will is fruitless, dispersed
Like hollowed-out blueberries thrown from the balcony

Marcel Wormsley

Over the crooked ledge of broken time,
Shattered like brittle hourglasses.

Her hand.

Long

separated

from

the

tethers

of

my

childhood

memories.

Damned unto perpetual submission I lay, here,
In the Sun's repose, in this cold hiatus of wind and song,
Alone, treading these fields of limitless vacuity,
In search of answers, in pursuit of finality.
I reason vigorously, and continue to question in hopes of
attaining but the slightest
Foothold of understanding,
Attempting to provide a final stability to these
Warring edifices of emotion and thought.
But in their grandeur all my answers are obscured.
The more I reach out to clasp
The impalpable blessed hand of translucent processes
And infinitely revealed meanings,
The further away it retreats.
Its shielded bosom rejects my cries,
Pushing me back into the primordial depths of
Unreality, nothingness, undifferentiated with base elements.
All my fear, once cleverly played by flickering shadows on the wall,
Materialized and served in a handful of black dust.

In Search of Moonlit Crevices

Mother!

No longer can I rest my head on her faint promises of
Assurance and untroubled resolution,
As she smiles at me from that singular and glorious space
Forever beyond my reach,
Tattered red quilt still in hand.

Marcel Wormsley

In Search of Moonlit Crevices

Felt, but Unseen

Felt, but unseen.
Once again the
Striated beast moves beneath us,
Looking for new angels
To face down some demons of old.
Withered knolls creep quietly
And settle in fixed space,
And we wonder why the galaxies roam
And multiply so wantonly.
Hear the song of the legend
Who

Didn't die,
But whose passion transports us
To newer and gladder tidings.
It never occurred to us that
We hitchhiked on their tails
All this time.

Behold a summons to possibility
And a calling to account of new thought,
Of hands marked with perfectly aligned
Veins of experience
Clasped in prayer, trembling with delight
As the eyes face down unpaved roads
Lush with unbridled verdure

Punctuated by sinewy vines that crawl
Slowly, marking out each inch with
Perfection, love.

A posthumous love letter tumbles freely
Amid an unsure wind, but hopeful.
Time will surely read it, and in
The cool of a reassuring Dawn,
He will run impulsively until out of breath,
Stopping besides a lowered branch
To weep a little.
And to smile.
And live a little more.

Marcel Wormsley

Generally Speaking

Generally speaking,
The reasons are self-evident,
And multiplied with each passing day.

And days become the subjects of
Dreams parceled out to eternal possibility.
And we go back to see the stuff of them,

And are startled.
But persistence gnaws at the
Gown of the witness who

Braves the fearsome phantasm
Of uncertainty and merges into it,
As the droplet into the depths of a luminous pond.

Tomorrow we will become
As baby eagles verging
On the precipice of hopes.

We will launch into multitudinous corridors
And emerge with shifting traces of glory
And affection on our wings.

Lest we become disoriented,
The illumination of translucent hearts will
Guide us through reasons hitherto unseen

But lived out through purpose,
Reified through reflection,
Embraced by trembling arms that do not seek to know,

But to feel, presently.

We Dangled

We dangled
From insistent shadows
With uniform fingers.

Leapt across yawning
Interstices of moments
Barely closed in on themselves,

Knee-deep in molten latticework
We may adjourn here
For the while.

We recall stories of
Nascent stones, completely dry
And brittle to the touch.

We will eat them,
And will roll about the
Contours of these meadows

Awash in the coolness
Of a dawn sanctified
By its own forgetfulness.

Marcel Wormsley

The Spirit Makes Its Rounds

The Spirit makes its rounds,
It warbles and gyrates.
It graces my hand.
It bends, glides, swishes,
Drains.

But it doesn't see me, yet.
For I am not ready.
It will come back soon.
And then it will engulf me,

Perhaps while I am asleep.

Run!

I am on the lam.

My glory.
Everywhere I go I am pursued.
I am a self-perpetuating offense.
I must escape.
Funny farm, but with no cows or jokes,
Just cold brick, locked doors, high fences and stifled dreams.
And needles too.
Can't get away from here.

A little girl recounts a sad, lowly tale of a lost slipper.
A dapper little pink and white marshmallow she is.
Insignificant.
I am frustrated.
So is she by the way her face cringes grotesquely
Like a hybrid angel-goblin.
But her story matters. Does mine? To another?
Visited by Lazar the rep,
with whom I had spoken to earlier on the phone.
Sound familiar?
Taller than I took him to be.
Lean with an aura of self-imposed dignity.
The smell of his lambskin coat intoxicates me.
A clean, brisk, tight musk permeates my soul.
I was busy at the time.
Roxanna, ah yes, she has a story as well.
She has grown into a voluptuous jardinière,
Topped with a bit of perky aplomb that arouses.
Everyone has a damn story.

Someone responded to me finally.
Taken apparently by my obscure wit.
Quitting this guy's church, my offering is paltry,
But he didn't have to make it known to everyone.
A gaunt man with robotic features wearing a jacquard apron
Trails me wherever I go.

Marcel Wormsley

Too bad I am stuck here in this place with him.
"Do they know you in this place," he asks.
Getting late, time for a little shopping.
A sepia-toned silhouette at the checkout window
Engaged in a spirited conversation
Tith an attentive and apprehensive other.
'Tis the end of something (school, work, freedom, not sure).
Got into a fight with P.J. from grade school.
A hulking mammoth of a man.
Still has that lazy eye.
I'll fain give him another.
Oh yeah and that other P.J. needed his ass kicked as well.
That crimson beast,
That moose-eyed supercilious bohemian outdoorsy son-of-a-bitch.
Yeah, that one.
How crazy is that!
Damn, late for class. Not gonna take the test.
Screw it.

Janice singing and testifying,
Taking up the whole sermon with her greasy gesticulations,
Her sanctimonious theatrics.
Give her a stage for the Pharisees.
Old Buzz from the call center clowns around in the seat next to me.
Flirting with some corpulent bubble of a woman
With studded nails, as if it mattered.
Some resistance there.
I give up.
Damn late for class again.
No work to turn in either.
Eight weeks behind.
A year and nothing to show for it.
Hardly anyone on the big six-wheeled multi-passenger Cadillac today.
Probably because yesterday was a holiday.
Most are still in varying stages of recovery.
I see, I see...Hey wait a sec!
Why the hell am I driving this animal?
I'm a bit nervous.
Swerving but maintaining control.
Steady as she goes!

In Search of Moonlit Crevices

My nerves are wracked; my hole in the heart has gotten wider.
So wide that it is violated at will by spirits with oblique intentions.
Heather from the hospital shares her story.
I like her story the best.
What an adorable woman.
I cannot resist.
I want to melt into her faster than an ice cube
Cast into the springs of Hades (a nice vacation spot I hear).
Furious.
I am going from classroom to classroom,
Picking off guileless soldiers and soldierettes,
And those who dare to get in my way.
I am a machine, again.
This time for real.
Or maybe not.
Where's my piece?
It may not be here, but the intent is undeniable,
As my soul jerks back and forth with passion moving with the threat.
On offense.

Navy installation.
Half suited up, half in pajamas.
I don't care.
Shosty's string quartet number 8.
A beautiful tragedy for the beautiful people.
Maybe for the exceptional among the base-born as well.
They are after me again.
Same half-renovated building, same rickety elevators.
Same metallic taste of tap water.
15th floor, no 16th is safer.
Less exposure, but harder getting down.
Nowhere is safe.
Prescription drug recall?
You can't be serious.
Insolent service rep (who isn't?)
Forms to sign.
Maybe I'm leaving after all.
Can't walk straight.
I think I left my neurons in a mason jar on the LCSW's desk.
This desk is new.
New staffer too. Very articulate.
I am probably safe now, or probably all the closer to destiny.

Marcel Wormsley

An old man to my right is going through the same rounds as I am.
Not so alone anymore.
Not so pursued I guess.
Apartments, the paint fumes are bold, robust,
But I still kiss them like I would have kissed Heather.
Tree-lined streets.
Baby Jonathan is all of three now.
Can't believe so much has passed.
He's so cooperative now, and smart too.

Marcel Wormsley

I Have Awaited Your Arrival

I have awaited your arrival
With anticipation and acid.

Douse this body
I have prepared for you
With both, until the color of pain begins to show.

Stretch it vigorously
Until its knees begin
To give way.

Journey until success is no more,
And walls begin to crumble.
Make known my nakedness

Unto an unsuspecting Moon.
Burn marks visible.

Excise Me from Your Womb

Excise me from your womb
And guide me through
Shifting plenitudes of dust
Redolent of those jagged moments
When fiery wreaths were hung in silence
But still ruled the day.

Sift me, then scatter me on all sides
As your lips begin to blow and cast
My name into deciduous glass
And candied trees that refuse to melt.
Make way for tomorrow
When toothless gnomes make love
As universal peace awakens,

Walks to the Sun and back,
Sits down and thinks itself blind.

Marcel Wormsley

Say Without Feeling

Say without feeling,
Do without knowing,
Intimacy gently seeped through the door
Lapped upon our footstep.
Sing when the valley subsides
And hidden dust becomes
Our recompense
For not being.

In Love with Weightlessness and Shadow

In love with weightlessness and shadow.
Figured with nothingness and unmolded light.
Dreamt once, but never fully conformed
Unto this world or the previous.

Sing tonight, or rest among the giants
Of solemn defiance,
And know thy specter within my dying glance,
Infinite to naught, porous in every direction,

Seeping blindly out of captivity.

Marcel Wormsley

A Thought Emerges

A thought emerges.
A swift burst
Of lurid incandescence
Smells of wood wetted by
Furious rain
And hoarse cackling
Stirred amid errant coughs
Boiled to warring shadows.

Perhaps the price to be paid
For the luxury
Of daytime revelry
Rests in the quotidian
Menace of skies
Progressively blinded by
Ripped hosiery and
Half-smiles that rarely
Importune our forgiveness.

And the thought is no more,
Whisked away by everything
Directionless (yet conscientious)
And now we stand proudly,
Warriors of the blackened meadow
Giving way to an empty sea.
We are infinitely torn,
But thrice bound,

To remembrance of Day,
To Glory feigned and true,
To heavy breathing
Punctuated by infrequent
Gasps of abandoned laughter.

Silence, and Magic Will Obtain

Silence, and magic will obtain
In small steps.
A handful of light
Is the cure for the abyss of a hollow spirit.

Finely-crafted footsteps intermingle with
Subtle twitches of the eye
Refusing blindness.
Doubt is a jaded bird with unleavened wings

That flies within range of the vengeful and the ravaged.
How many pieces remain
Of the original pulchritude forlorn,
The smiles that once incited growth through

Tenderness and restraint?
The beloved writhes and begins to glow
Like incinerated dust,
Its flowers turned into themselves in shame.

Glory will be had
In the past,
When the fog was new,
And it hugged you timidly.

Marcel Wormsley

If We Go All the Way to the End

If we go all the way to the end,
Where will all our beginnings lie?
If your piecemeal heart ceases to rend,
Where will all your tears go to dry?

If nothingness is war,
Will our presence conjure peace?
As glistening bodies wash ashore
Will our darkened conscience surcease?

Curse the wayward shadow, bruised and inconstant light!
Nebulous footsteps that seek terrain.
Absorb my gaze, until the taste of night,
And remember me, use me, in vain.

III

Before

It would be two years before
I would see you drifting there again
Arms ravaged and spread apart
Knowing and resisting

The hymn of the lotus
Who coursed our path
So many times before—
Wailing, suffering,

So that redemption may
Find and overtake us.
Consolation rounds the way
And becomes what we aspired to be

Back when your trembling hand
Took repose in my altar,
And the phantasmagoria of
Unlicensed touches

Dutifully escaped us.
Become still, my love,
And submerge your guilt
Into my aching abyss.

Decry not the glory of
Tattered saints in line to drink
From the abundant rivers
Of our forgotten travails.

Mold them into centers of incandescence
With wings glistened by
The silken nectar of our lust
And musings felt but unseen.

Marcel Wormsley

Space, Time, Distance

Our lines were drawn by buried affections
Gilded by quivering skins
That knew estrangement,
But that soon would find oneness

On a path illumined only by
Light that space had abandoned.
Repose had ceased to placate the weary
Even when the journey seemed unbroken

And the hours fell back upon their slopes.
We will refuse to sigh until
The dusk of negation is suspended,
Until I can feel all your promises

Slithering in my thickened hand,
Restless as the leaves aflutter,
Witness to moments that danced until prostration
Even while the stars began to wonder in our direction.

The Moon Scarcely Remembers the Night

The moon scarcely remembers the night
When the valley wept for once
And dissolved into fragments of
Supple guilt and free-roaming sorrow.

The next tide impresses with shades of
Forced introspection,
Of enslaved moths and the incumbent flame.
Knowing becomes obsolete

When the final disposition awakens
And the lessons of yore are rewritten
In translucent blood.
Save me, Oh Specter of impending

Timelessness, from the clash of
Hope and Doom,
From which eventide will surely erect
A fortress so noble that this legion of

Unblinking twilight will disrobe and entreat for mercy,
And the warlocks will follow suit
As they prepare to be ravished by
Fallen angels with wings usurped by

Undulating visions of tomorrow.

Marcel Wormsley

Sweet Resignation

Sweet resignation,
And all that needed to be said
Funneled into my chest
With a touch of liquid resentment.
Joy calls out beyond the edifice
Of vain thoughts.
Weltschmerz is a boiling stream that
Runs through the swarthy
Steppes of frozen sky.

Name one reason to
Sing the tunes of rats and
Transform them into fairies,
And I will give you my words,
Followed by my darkened vision.
Losing earth is a lot like
Making love unbalanced,
Jolts of fire and recompense
Interspersed with naked heavings
Quickly sated without cause or method.

Abduct my memories
And carve them into sprightly wings.
Before I take flight,
Dedicate my listless heart to
The city's edge,
Where some yearnings failed to sprout,
And others continue to grow.
Remember the dusty pathway to the
Only open window to the
House on moonlit creek.

Branches

Quietly we dwell in our secret places
And carry on nameless,
Forbidden from likeness,
And then a branch falls to the meadow below,
Bursting into multifarious little pieces,
Complex and diversified,

Each bearing a misshapen face
With eyes desperately gasping for something lovely again,
Or at least stable and unshifting and without pain.
Mouths have crumbled into serrated grimaces
That do not speak.

They must number in the millions now,
Whirling, bobbing and cracking beneath our feet.
We kick them away, but they return
More frenzied and grotesque as ever.
Soon they will consume us whole

And we will suffocate under their weight.
We will bear faint visions of fingers interlocked
And voices lifted in togetherness
That will soon dissipate into the unremitting thinness
Of eternal sequestration.

What is the Promised land but an island of rank desolation,
Populated by naught but a vast canopy of naked men
Reduced to categories, bound together by ropes and chains
Lying prostrate in the sun?

Where will this child go to find shelter from a broken womb,
Pierced by the branches that continue to fall?
The old woman will surely speak life into this lost seed
Once she arises from the dust of darkened corners
And partial skulls set aflame by idle hands.

Marcel Wormsley

Hate we knew not, until our tree had fallen.
We are alone, bereft of even the gentlest of litanies.
A sigh lingers for a moment, then disappears.
A wrinkled black hand trembles, then stops.
An angel weeps in the distance.

Marcel Wormsley

Take My Final Utterance

Take my final utterance
and disperse it below,
avoiding the mention of heathens
hanging by the edges of
denuded moonlights and visions
steeped in worry for the possibility
that refused the piercing psalm
of the one-eyed cockcrow.

Consume this docile flower
with my laughter in mind,
and the slight stroke of your hand
against where my face used to be.
Recall the quiet sway of brittle trees
poised for celebratory gyrations
in honor of disjointed myths
and weather-beaten pantheons

of mindless gods.

From This Vantage

From this vantage
We have quelled our devils,
Torn our veils,
And dozed off in the effulgence of Being.

For a time our hopes were recycled,
Our superstitions dashed,
Our reach for life extended into
Flashes of distilled desperation

For a gentle upsurge that drifts and transforms,
That subsides and appears again
Ever-more slight, ever-more humble,
Dallying effortlessly with rambling thoughts along the
embankment.

Marcel Wormsley

This Place

There is life here.

And there are seeds aflutter with
Gleeful songs and abstracted praises.
And a blind bacchante coruscates with abandon,
Dancing amid a night's earnest welcome;
And children enthralled by oblivion,
Bought and sold by insular moments.

Here is a toast to a passing frame,
Of many a breath drawn, and taken away,
Of an eye for nicety at times,
And at times given to bland, tawdry components
Hastily-refined (for my conscience).

To a past extolled
This new perspective
Determines unforeseen positions,
Clarity of vision,
Decrepit memories of
Mistakes buried into misplaced oaths.

I seek the fugitive in all permanence,
Then I cloak it in aureate trappings
Of meandering satin.
This fervor bears witness
And is steeped in tonight's rage.
But I love her
Albeit with bruised and disconsolate
Prayers yet to be uttered.

Marcel Wormsley

In Time

We shall reflect upon the meaning of our disgrace,
Grasping truth unencumbered by blinded eyes.
Fugitive moments eagerly await the call of memory's trace,
To stand before the day duly countenanced by obscurity's demise.
We'll hasten to discard every cloak and vain disguise,
And submit to all that the interest of honesty requires.
We'll journey through forbidden caves
of deceit and compromise,
Abducting strange thoughts, denuding secluded desires.
Fate guards the door of timeless secrecy
to which our crime aspires,
Every path to resistance impeded by overgrown weeds of shame,
Ravished by the guilt that remains long after the fact expires,
We kneel wearily at the feet of judgment,
ignominious passions with no name.
We are what virtue has disavowed.
We are what freedom has disallowed.

Marcel Wormsley

A Spindle Emerges

A spindle emerges
And worlds retreat into unknowing
On all sides.
The vortex has been reborn
And it figures into the life of spaces
Turgid with the fallen heroes of reminiscence
And motion inflamed.

And around it goes,
Taking time with it and dissolving it
Into hollow particles that move along
Slightly curved corridors
One by one, after a fashion.
And blackened thoughts
Begin to coalesce.

The corridors straighten out
And empty into vacuums of potential being
Sealed by a single, winding thread of excess darkness
Occasionally punctuated by iridescent
Moments of awareness.
Clarity happens best when edges are
Seared and smoothed out,

Connected by the wings of galactic angels
And cosmic vagabonds that sprint in every direction.
Tonight they will all break free
And be seen no more.
The vortex will be shattered and consumed,
Spaces will bend until collapse,
But memories will resume, fully-realized, on all sides.

Feel the Pangs of the Restive Heath

Feel the pangs of the restive heath
below your feet
That nightly howl for aught
but whatever was conceived
unaware of freedom,
unquiet in sorrow,
perpetually a moment removed
from the next climax
followed by understanding.

Great is the hope that finds its place
in the ever-widening vortex of
unquiet crescents and honeyed arias,
reaching out and contracting,
interconnected on all sides,
blind but frozen into a knowing gaze
that sits quietly at the edge of the lake
still not quite forgetting.

Marcel Wormsley

Trace My Steps Knowingly...

Trace my steps knowingly
with your whispered incantations.
See me to the crest
and look down on the terrace
they have carved out for us.

What of tenderness remains
in the subdued glory of lowly pastures
whose only wish was to fortify
the outstretched arms of chance
and the ploughman's lament?

Redemption lies just beneath the surface
of impassioned passes to and fro,
of weathered hopes and copious returns.
Fruit beckons becoming as old iniquities are put to rest.
A procession of future mornings looks back over its shoulder
and shivers in wistful delight.

Requiem after a Dream

It all commenced with a journey to the edge of shadows
cast forth by a trace of light that smiled and imparted to me
truths that seemed to persist throughout eons;
Between one eon and the next a steady look speaks
directly into my Being, causing it to stir
with naïve inquiries into the state and manner of its origin.

And the Sun began to recline
possibly to fill in the gaps of lost space,
arresting every silken prayer in its wake.
An incandescent strand of her hair binds
it all together. I grab a portion and
waltz across worlds misshapen at the poles

And elongated at the center.
Her symphony arises breezily from the hazy blue
moldings that encase the equatorial seas
coursing throughout this protracted belly
of affections and passions unalloyed and unmasked.
A demigoddess once envied her tears

And attempted to destroy them,
but was distracted by the exigencies of every mangled thought
that swelled within, aching for emancipation,
begging the heart to recall every shrill note sung by
this restless hoard of deeply-perturbed, jaundiced crows
soon to drown mercilessly in her elegant streams.

Every angle has patiently waited outside of time, looking in,
awaiting her return. From whence will she come?
How long will they sing her praises before they glare into her windows,
erupting the seas of my solace anew?
Behold! Her silhouette glistens at the darkest hour.
She won't weep this time; but will nourish me with the

Marcel Wormsley

Honeyed nectar of her voice,
which glows once ingested, then dissolves into a million questions
all asked and answered, interlocked and melded together
with slippery edges that taper off every eventide.
And every morning the journey begins again,
tracing a long, serpentine path into the shadow's edge,

Addled by the piecemeal memory of her kisses,
Filled to surfeit with the lustful ambrosia of her
secrets disclosed under the hushed bend of this crescent glow
that shimmers no more. The rain has made it dull;
A memory dangles and fades into a patchwork of speckled flowers,
slightly recumbent, pointed in the direction
where her footsteps would have been.

Marcel Wormsley

Anatomy of a Tear

Formless and inconstant paths,
weighted roots with no foundation;
whence does it arise but from a
disjointed countenance with no proportion,
or a leaf from a broken branch?

Dust in the fields,
sunless clouds in aimless procession,
breathless winds and incorporeal birds
that have forgotten their wings;
the water's edge no longer beckons.

The once gentle and complaisant calf limps away in fear
along a scabrous meadow that has turned in unto itself,
where the borders now fold into jagged embankments on all sides,
where the drought-weakened oak palliates no more
and the hope of a thousand tomorrows goes to rest

Face down, arms tucked in,
like a child stroked gently by the lapping shore.
Fate has made its final trek across the mound
and now comes to compel my love,
to usurp my longings and make sprightly
each of my steps to a sweet place beneath

A darkened moon where the leaves are heard no more,
where the touch has faded and this thoughtless mass
has swallowed the desiderium of yesteryear's solace.
A singular drop seeks nothingness but does not find.
It vacillates between atonement and quietude

As have all the drops before it,
as have the senescent imaginings of an unattainable peace
that broods just below a smiling face.
I will not see it fall to the earth below;
The eyes have chosen the undifferentiated sky,
and the sky, the unseen.

In Search of Moonlit Crevices

Release

All that torment has loved has disappeared,
and we remain hopeful.
The significance of her efforts
have not gone unnoticed; indeed,
they have recapitulated old victories
and insights that had been hitherto obscured
by notions unseen and ideations to come.
We rally together for a promise of worlds to be

And fully satiate our desire for sanity
by committing to novel patterns of doing and breathing
deeper and more profound
as if the air we knew all along turned in on itself
and proclaimed that only the decadent shadow
could partake of her beauty.
We do not hope for redemption; it is irrelevant.
We do not participate in the vagaries of mindlessness

As we have already been thrice illumined by chariots
sallying forth in a devil's mist.
After all, we have connected eons ago by the
hands of molecular consistencies and arrangements,
morphed into ornaments of a quiet and intricate despair,
became ripe for contemplation and eventual division,
and ennobled by a distinction not quite unlike
that we have seen in the old woman by the sea,

Who recalls those she instilled with benedictions and protections,
those who knew nothing of the imminent graying of the cloud,
or the sable rainfall in late winter,
or the cellular dance taking place in her furrowed hand.
We knew she didn't exist as a fullness or even a drop of contingency,
but Fate would make it clear that this handmaiden of the gods
had no choice but to enjoin the waves to cease,
the moon to readjust and the whispers to become

Marcel Wormsley

Psalms of renewal and purpose.
Perhaps when I awaken from my slumber,
I shall call upon the disenchantment of the lost,
and be reunited with my passion for the nuance of colored thoughts
in a colorless world. I will know breath anew,
and each movement toward being will ripen
throughout successive periods of clarity and understanding.
It is then that I will become ingrained in myself,
and project in infinite directions.

And There I Stood

And there I stood
at the threshold of infinity,

wondering when
the tides would cease to swerve,

when the moon would
turn to face me and weep,
when the lighthouse
would become darkened

by the sempiternal emptiness
of unanswered questions.

And then I chose a star to hold,
to cherish and protect as the path takes on new direction.

I speak to a destiny that radiates possibility,
that dissipates the tribulations of yore

and casts them into the pond
where I once thought the answers awaited me.

And here I sing robust melodies
bejeweled with red stones,

warm and smooth to the touch,
filled with a luscious silence, a knowing.

The future reveals an exploding genesis,
its particulates raining upon my head

down my face, attached to my song,
christened by the scintillations

emanating from my bosom.

Marcel Wormsley

In Search of Moonlit Crevices

Resting Solitude

Resting solitude,
beware the quivering hand of Night's mercenary
and the muted helical wisps
of sweet despair that well-nigh consume
the flesh of innocence.

Lurid reflections recovered throughout
the travails of unrelenting circular journeys
foretell stories of transcendence and of sorrow,
and of leaves waxing restful on the pond's silent breast.
Protean skies sit god-like on their thrones,

Heads bowed but shifting anxiously.
The roots of these edifices will grow, they say,
and in due time, beatified to soaring ecstasy,
where children will lead in song,
and tread the dusky streets as Kings and Queens.

Marcel Wormsley

Lavender Reveries

Lavender reveries
concomitant with swift movements
around, then through, then around again,
never to return to their places of emergence,
but to keep striving and transcending,
until they become as one,
and the ego is vanquished.
And a remnant graces her quivering visage,
wholly and concertedly renewed
by a tender lattice of divine thought,
in which the movements slow,
and the colors dissipate in the space of a blink,
and all that is left is a Barmecidal trance
of a thousand ages,
where the fruitful have come to keep vigil
and pray until the Sun turns gray.

Where the Rivers Converge

Meet me where the rivers converge,
where the elemental

upsurge

of thought and reflection
begin to inspire

the formation

of territories newly populated
by the wisdom of

hands that prayed

themselves into warm bundles
of anxious grins that called upon the old

incantations

of lost serpents, mighty but humble
and for the most part without guile

voiceless...

but keenly aware of the changes in direction
and flow, and contemporary with outgrowths of

new being

not yet reduced by the apparitions we have yet to fight.

Marcel Wormsley

Absorbed Space

Absorbed space,
where the branches met their
reflections
and
her solace
birthed itself from eternal hiding,

Where the minions of fate
worked in concert
to don
the ornamented veil
of futures subsequently
resisted,

Where drops of sky
chased
a soulless moon
to its final appearance,
returning to
the fringes of darkened hours.

Tremble Not

Tremble not
when the forest of extreme
desire
becomes overgrown,
when the trees pant and beg
for eyes that never
blinked
during
a moment of caprice,
when pulsating
worlds became intertwined
and flowers laced
with
traces of virgin earth.

Marcel Wormsley

I've Heard the Echoes

I've heard the echoes,
chased the shadows,
danced with the reveries
of phantom caresses.
Retreat with me
to a safe space
'neath the snow-laden burrows
behind the curtain of remembrances
where we will carve out
the annals
of innocence and mirth,
and ascend the smoky hills by night's end.

Nestled by the Fireside

Nestled by the fireside,
listening.
The temperate caress
of an errant flicker
awakens the latent
serenade of the season,
carrying expectant smiles
to their place beyond the sphere.

Everything exists
in this series of nows and forevers,
in the way your hand
Lies untroubled in mine,
redolent of the halcyon's
repose after her flight
through celestial reveries
interconnected by the vestal melodies
of winged seraphs
perched atop the star that sits aloof
bearing our likeness.

Marcel Wormsley

And Then There was Heaven

And then there was Heaven,
you never thought
we would see this vestigial
glimmer of a thousand wanderers,
each with extended hands
in search of fullness, or nothing.
Distraught is a stranded
dove coruscating with abandoned
memories of a love unraveled
with a sweet kind of pain,
no less than the way my good nights
are ravished by thoughts of
staying put, of enduring her final touch.

And It Was Wonder

And it was wonder
that had spoken
as we swayed gently
down the path of
remnant hopes;
after courage abandoned us
and the fruits of shadowy
countenances enamored our
malleable hearts,

where innocence
pressed onward towards
incremental sacrifices
and blind passions from somewhere
immemorial,
where tokens
of estrangement and grief
fell from the celestial sphere
of wanton pride
and unrequited joys.

We never knew
and yet have always known.
At once. In absentia and below
the commoner's footsteps.
We knew of the crumpled letters
and molten brass pendants.
We saw the birth of sweet chrysanthemums
whirling along the rustic meadow,
the chant of naked salvation
where no utterance had dared crossed.

The end will not emerge
as the benevolent monk
from the wooden haze,
but as the flock of doves
rightly divided among themselves,
according to various hues
in their wings.

Marcel Wormsley

She Arrived Bearing Leaflets

She arrived bearing leaflets
gathered hastily from a tree
that once made its home
along the bluff that bowed
in the direction of All Saint's Creek,

Where the flightless seraphs would
traverse from time to time
to retrace the melody
that escaped somewhere between
celestial monuments immemorial

And the hallowed confluence of
electric mists and vernal shadows
that marked the beginning
and the end of a journey's refrain,
just beyond the bend.

One leaf was given to a man of great wisdom
who preferred the wistful caress
of remote breezes emanating from
solitude sweetened with age
and fortified with crystalline shells of Faith.

Another was given to the golden-haired urchin
who painted the meadows with colors
birthed out of fond remembrances of
tender passages from lullabies
that dared to trace their lineage back to Blue.

Several more were given to
the animals that dutifully roamed
the forgotten stretch of the forest
in which visions of sunrise trickled down
like nervous rain on its journey beneath the surface.

In Search of Moonlit Crevices

The last leaf was given to me
as I wondered into the chestnut stream
that flowed from her eyes.
I held it to my heart and promised her
that I would awaken each morning hereafter

Bearing lavender periwinkles for her silken hair
extending in every direction, culminating into
tightly-woven star steps leading back
to the beginning of the Creek
where there were dreams of flight, patient and graceful.

I promised her that when the leaf crumbles,
my heart will divide the pieces among
every meandering soul in search of her lament,
and legions of despondent youth
will arise and build spatial arias from her maiden cry.

And the galaxies will awaken, changing form
with each resolution, presaging the moment
when each star will descend upon the horizon
and illuminate the spot where the leaflets once
graced her outstretched hand.

I sit and mark the journey
of lost stars that find their way down the bluff
and into my bosom, where I inscribe her smile on them,
and turn them into wings that glow in the dark
for the angels who plant trees at night.

Marcel Wormsley

This Recumbent Hour

This recumbent hour
casts a lurid glare
of unconcern
over the great tidings
and celebratory
appurtenances of olden soirees

where
the evening breeze
kneels down
and renders obeisance
to a forgotten night
in confirmation of
glory, however tenuous.

The path never seeks
its own length,
nor the mirage
its reflection.
We are left with a vague
awareness of a lonely Sunday
emerging from the hearth
of flagrant hearts
awaiting the promise of
dissolution.

Forms

Poise is how she carries
the weight of the world (love)
upon her shoulders so effortlessly
as an ethereal emptiness
dutifully traces her form's soft edges
and surrounds them with a fullness
just outside of time and light.

Behold,
a silkened sillouhette
Mother Grace has sprinkled with crystalline confections
glistening
in every direction -
outward and inward -
once upon a rose velvet Moon
whose axis of rotation
kept the world's weight
elevated and ascending
in the hollow expanse
of her every moment,
from her primordial incarnations
unto the heavenly instant
my eyes were graced by her
tender smile.

A forest awakens once and for all time,
pulsating with her energy spirals
in keeping with the rhythm of
those lunar hearts swirling ever upwards along her axis, admiring her
balance, still effortless,
even as the weight upon her shoulders increased,
and the vibrations around her
fluctuated with inconstancy
due to weariness.

Marcel Wormsley

The trees become alive,
branches limber and lithe,
swaying to her songs of
laughter and glee.
Leaves grow iridescent and scurry about
to approximate her borders,
statuesque and regal.
And then the dance begins,
"Alive with me," she demands,
as she takes my hand deeper into
this earthen metropolis,
where moth and dust dare not corrupt,
and thieves reclaim their virtue.

A flower looks up at the sky,
ornate with stars that illumine the path
to retrace her, over and over,
so that I do not stray from
the place where she became Queen
for the first time,
where she appeared in her
rose-imbued vestments
glowing in a mysterium of
sound and color separated
from all form and thought.

In my dreams she sits contentedly
beside a waterfall, the flow
subdued by the sweet harmonies
emanated by crimson patterns each
manifesting a path directly into the part of my heart where there is only
the joy I felt when her starlit eyes fixed upon mine,
where her honeyed skin
reflected the tender kisses of a thousand Suns
as her silhouette took form
for the first time,
where the forest dance never ended,
where the lustrous strands of her hair stream forth in concert
with every waterfall, pouring out into an endless sea
of rose petals I picked for her,
punctuated by tides that carry the dance to the place
where the last star in the cosmos sits quietly,
hoping that she will visit it one day, and give it an axis of light,
so that it too can dance,
and laugh with her,
and become form again.

In Search of Moonlit Crevices

What Manner of Soul

What manner of soul
reaches out
from the dust
of living under the
illusion of freedom?

Where do the poppies go
to replenish their relevance,
their contract with
the vulgar steps
of a broken smile?

The imagination releases,
then contracts.
A world of elongated being
creeps in the windowless cellar,
just below the cobwebs and shadows.

The precipice has arisen
and called forth the
gods of munificent mercy,
to hold him back for a moment,
only to be released anew,

after the crow's pass,
and the once-dejected optimist
will gild his wings with icy luster,
determined to rise, beholden to none.

Marcel Wormsley

About the Author

Marcel is an author, poet, as well as a mental and behavioral health advocate. His professional interests lie in the cultivation and nurturing of human creative potential in order to promote healing, primarily through the exercise and process of writing poetry. Marcel's writing explores a variety of themes grounded in spiritual awareness and knowledge.

Visit his blog at marcelwormsley.com